Learn to Read Modern Hebrew in 5 Days

DAVID BEN ZAKEN

Copyright © 2015

Published by Wolfedale Press 2015

WOLFEDALE PRESS

All rights reserved. No part of this publication may be reproduced, distributed, or transmitted in any form or by any means, including photocopying, recording, or other electronic or mechanical methods, without the prior written permission of the publisher.

The cover image of Ein Gedi Beach, in Israel is licensed under cc by-sa 3.0. Author: Adiel lo

ISBN-13: 978-0-9959305-9-9

CONTENTS

Introduction	i
Unit 1 – ל, נ, מ, א	1
Unit 2 – ד, ג, י	3
Unit 3 – ר, ה, ת, ו	5
Unit 4 – ש, ב	7
Unit 5 – ט, ז, ס, כ	9
Unit 6 – צ, פ	11
Unit 7 – ק, ע, ח	13
Unit 8 – Review	15
Appendix – Vowels	17
Hebrew Alphabet	19
Glossary – Thematic Order	21
Glossary – Alphabetical Order	29

INTRODUCTION

Learning a new alphabet can be very intimidating for an English speaker only used to reading the Latin alphabet. This is partly why English speakers tend to stick to learning other languages that use the same alphabet, such as French, Spanish and Italian – because they seem a lot easier!

But learning a new alphabet does not have to be so difficult. Some alphabets, like Hebrew, can indeed be challenging for an English speaker. However, the real difficulty is finding a good system to learn the new alphabet so that the student does not get discouraged and give up before making any real progress. Making progress in the language is the best motivator.

The secret to learning a new alphabet is to be taught each letter separately, and then to practice how the new letters combine with letters you already know to read real words in the alphabet in a structured way. This is not revolutionary – it is probably how you learned to read English – but it is not easy to find for other languages.

This book will teach you how to read the Hebrew alphabet in exactly that way, and with this method you will be able to read Modern Hebrew in only 5 days or less! After that you will be able to enjoy the Hebrew language and culture in a way that you were never able to before.

THE HEBREW ALPHABET
אלף־בית עברי

The Hebrew alphabet contains 22 letters and is written from right to left. There is no difference between upper and lower case letters;

however 5 letters have different forms when used at the end of a word.

Vowels are not normally written in Modern Hebrew, although some consonants are used to represent long vowels. A system does exist to write all of the vowels. Called niqqud, this system consists of a series of dots and dashes written above and below the letters. This system is only used in special cases, however, such as in dictionaries and books for children, and not in normal publications.

The lack of written vowels, and the fact that some letters can be pronounced in more than one way, make the Hebrew alphabet challenging for beginners; it is not always clear by looking at a new word exactly how to pronounce it and often a dictionary or native speaker must be consulted. Remember, however, that this is also largely true for Modern English spelling and pronunciation and much like English, after some practice and a feel for the language, reading Modern Hebrew becomes much easier.

The Modern Hebrew alphabet derives from a stylized "square" version of the Aramaic script that was used in the Persian Empire during the 3rd century BCE. This alphabet was also used in the Jewish diaspora communities around the world, and used to write the various Jewish vernacular languages that developed, such as Yiddish and Ladino.

This course focuses on Modern Hebrew as spoken in the state of Israel. Despite this focus, the course will still be very useful for students interested in the Biblical form of Hebrew. After learning to read Hebrew with this course, reading Biblical Hebrew will come much easier – the alphabet is the same.

HOW TO USE THIS COURSE

The primary goal of this course book is to teach the reader to recognize the Hebrew alphabet and begin to read the Modern Hebrew language.

The principal way this is accomplished is by teaching the individual pronunciations of each letter, and then utilizing "Practice" sections where the student can practice reading real Hebrew words. These "Practice" sections are very important and the main way the student will start to feel comfortable with the Hebrew alphabet. The answers to all "Practice" questions are included directly below the questions, but try to avoid looking at the answers until you have attempted to answer the questions yourself.

Throughout the book, the reader will learn approximately 150 real Modern Hebrew words. These words were carefully selected to be of maximum benefit to beginner students of the language. In the end of the book there are two glossaries – one in thematic order and one in alphabetical order – where one can study and memorize all the words learned in this course

The course material has been designed to be completed slowly over 5 days, while reviewing lessons as necessary. You are encouraged to go at whatever pace you feel comfortable with and to feel free to go back to lessons to review as much as needed.

Good luck and I hope you enjoy the first step on your journey to learning the Hebrew language.

UNIT 1 - א, מ, נ, ל

In Modern Israeli Hebrew, the letter א, called aleph, has no real pronunciation of its own and is used to represent the vowel that is attached to it. When a word begins with a vowel sound, it is always written with a א in Hebrew. Although this can be any vowel, beginners can start by assuming א is a long "a" sound. א is also sometimes used to indicate a glottal stop, meaning a pause or a catch in the throat between two vowel sounds, like in "uh-oh" (IPA: /ʔ/). This glottal stop will be represented by ' in the pronunciation in this book.

The letter מ, called mem, is pronounced like the "m" in "man" or "me" (IPA: /m/). מ has a slightly different form, called mem sofit, when used at the end of a word. The sofit form is ם.

The letter נ, called nun, is pronounced like the "n" in "now" or "Nancy (IPA: /n/). נ also has a sofit form used at the end of words. The sofit form is ן.

The letter ל, called lamed, is pronounced like the "l" in "little" or "like" (IPA: /l/).

Short vowels are not usually written in Modern Hebrew. This means that you often have to know how the word is pronounced before you can read it properly. This is not a problem for native speakers because they already speak the language. To illustrate what this is like for native speakers imagine if English followed the same principal. Can you read this sentence?

Modrn Hebrw is nt dffclt to read

As you can see it is not too difficult - but this is a challenge for foreign learners of Hebrew, especially beginners.

PRACTICE

Try to read these English words in their Hebrew disguise. Remember that the words are written right to left and that short vowels are not written. The English words are given below.

1. מן
2. לם
3. נאנא
4. לאן

ANSWERS

1. man (or men)
2. lamb
3. Nana
4. lawn

UNIT 2 - ד, ג, י

The letter י, called yod, is pronounced like the "y" in "yes" or "yellow" (IPA: /j/). It is also used for the long "ee" sound in "bee" or the "i" in "spaghetti" (IPA /i/). Think of this letter the same as the English letter "y" which can be pronounced as a consonant like in "yellow" or as a vowel like in "tiny". Also like the English "y", when a word begins with י it is always pronounced as a consonant. In this book this letter will be represented as either "y" or "i" depending on pronunciation.

The letter ג, called gimel, is pronounced like the "g" sound in "good" or "goose" (IPA: /g/).

The letter ד, called dalet, is pronounced like the "d" sound in "dad" or "David" (IPA: /d/).

PRACTICE

Try to read these real Modern Hebrew words. The English translation is given next to each word. The correct pronunciations are given in the answers below.

1. יד (hand/arm)
2. דם (blood)
3. יין (wine)
4. ים (sea)
5. מאי (May)
6. ידיד (friend)
7. אדם (man)
8. ילד (boy)

3

9. דג (fish)
10. אגם (lake)

ANSWERS

1. yad
2. dam
3. yayin
4. yam
5. may
6. yadid
7. adam
8. yeled
9. dag
10. agam

UNIT 3 - ו, ת, ה, ר

The letter ו, called vav, is pronounced like the "v" sound in "very" (IPA: /v/). This letter is also used to represent long vowels. In Modern Hebrew, ו can be pronounced either as the "u" sound in "glue" (IPA: /u/), or as the "o" sound in "hope" (IPA /o/). If the optional dotted forms are shown, the letter is pronounced "u" with the dot to the left side (וּ) and "o" with the dot above (וֹ). However since the dots are not normally written, a beginner will have to consult the pronunciation to see if the word is pronounced with a "u" or an "o".

The letter ת, called tav, is pronounced like the "t" sound in "ten" (IPA /t/).

The letter ה, called he, is pronounced like the "h" in "home" (IPA /h/). At the end of a word, ה is not normally pronounced and instead shows that the word ends in an "ah" sound (similar to א at the beginning of a word).

The letter ר, called resh, is usually pronounced like a French "r" sound in Modern Hebrew (IPA /ʁ/). It is also sometimes pronounced the same as an English "r" sound, especially among English speakers in Israel.

TRY NOT TO CONFUSE

The letter ו and the sofit form of the letter nun from Unit 1, ן look very similar. The difference is that nun extends down below the line and the vav stops at the line. Remember ו is pronounced "v", "u" or "o" and ן is pronounced "n" and only used at the end of a word.

PRACTICE

Try to read these real Hebrew words. The English translation is given next to each word. The correct pronunciations are given in the answers below.

1. מָלוֹן (hotel)
2. אדום (red)
3. גדול (big)
4. יום (day)
5. היום (today)
6. אתמול (yesterday)
7. יהדות (Judaism)
8. נהר (river)
9. הר (mountain)
10. רגל (foot / leg)

ANSWERS

1. malon
2. adom
3. gadol
4. yom
5. hayom
6. etmol
7. yahadut
8. nahar
9. har
10. regel

UNIT 4 - ב, ש

The letter ב, called bet, is pronounced two different ways. It is either pronounced like the "b" sound in "bad" (IPA: /b/) or like the "v" sound in "very" (IPA /v/). When the optional dots are shown it is clear which pronunciation to use; without a dot (ב), it is pronounced "v" and with a dot (בּ), it is pronounced "b".

Unfortunately the dots are almost never written. Beginners should get used to the pattern that if ב is written at the beginning of a word, or the beginning of a syllable, it is usually pronounced "b" and if ב is written in the middle or the end of a word it is usually pronounced "v".

The letter ש, called shin, is also pronounced two different ways. In texts where the dots are shown, the dot on the top left (שׂ) signifies that the letter is pronounced like the "s" in "simple" (IPA: /s/) and the dot on the top right (שׁ), signifies that it is pronounced like the "sh" sound in "she" (IPA /ʃ/).

Unfortunately for beginners the dots are not written in most texts and whether the letter is pronounced "s" or "sh" does not follow any real pattern. The reader must therefore look up the pronunciation to determine if ש is pronounced "s" or "sh".

PRACTICE

Try to read these Hebrew words. The English translation is given next to each word. The correct pronunciations are given in the answers below.

1. בשר   (meat)
2. גבינה   (cheese)
3. בירה   (beer)
4. לבן   (white)
5. בן אדם   (person)
6. אב   (father)
7. אשה   (woman)
8. שמלה   (dress)
9. ראש   (head)
10. גשם   (rain)
11. שלג   (snow)
12. שמש   (sun)

ANSWERS

1. basar
2. g'vina
3. bira
4. lavan
5. ben adam
6. av
7. isha
8. simla
9. rosh
10. geshem
11. sheleg
12. shemesh

UNIT 5 - כ, ס, ז, ט

The letter כ, called kaf, is pronounced two different ways. It is either pronounced like the "k" sound in "kick" (IPA: /k/) or like the "ch" sound in the German "doch" (IPA /x/). This second sound is the throat clearing guttural sound that is a distinct part of the Hebrew language and should be practiced by beginners. This sound will be represented by "kh" in the pronunciation.

When the dots are written, כ is pronounced "k" and כ is pronounced "kh", but since the dots are rarely written, note that the pattern is if כ is written at the beginning of a word, or the beginning of a syllable, it is usually pronounced "k" and if כ is written in the middle or the end of a word it is usually pronounced "kh". כ also has a sofit form, used at the end of a word, which looks like ך.

The letter ס, called samekh, is pronounced like the "s" sound in "son" (IPA /s/).

The letter ז, called zayin, is pronounced like the "z" sound in "zoo" (IPA /z/).

The letter ט, called tet, is pronounced like the "t" sound in "town" (IPA /t/). In Modern Hebrew this letter is pronounced the same as ת.

TRY NOT TO CONFUSE

The letter ד, called dalet from Unit 3, resembles the new letter kaf in its sofit form ך. The difference is that sofit kaf extends down below the writing line and the dalet stop at the line.

Remember ד is pronounced "d" and ך is pronounced "kh" at the end of a word.

PRACTICE

Try to read these Hebrew words. The English translation is given next to each word. The correct pronunciations are given in the answers below.

1. רכבת (train)
2. מכונית (car)
3. בית כנסת (synagogue)
4. כן (yes)
5. כלב (dog)
6. מטוס (airplane)
7. סירה (boat)
8. אוזן (ear)
9. זול (cheap)
10. טוב (good)
11. אוכל (food)
12. כיסא (chair)

ANSWERS

1. rekevet
2. m'khonit
3. beit knesset
4. ken
5. kelev
6. matos
7. sira
8. ozen
9. zol
10. tov
11. okhel
12. kise

UNIT 6 - פ, צ

The letter פ, called pe, is pronounced in two different ways. It is either pronounced like the "p" sound in "pepper" (IPA: /p/) or like the "f" sound in "far" (IPA /f/). When the dots are written the "p" pronunciation carries the dot (פּ).

Since the dots are rarely written, the pattern to remember is that if פ is written at the beginning of a word, or the beginning of a syllable, it is usually pronounced "p" and if פ is written in the middle or the end of a word it is usually pronounced "f". פ also has a sofit form, used at the end of words, which looks like ף.

The letter צ, called tsadi, is pronounced like the "ts" sound in "lots" (IPA /ts/). Unlike English, in Hebrew this sound can begin a word as well as occur in the middle or the end of a word. צ also has a sofit form, used at the end of words, which looks like ץ.

PRACTICE

Try to read these Hebrew words. The English translation is given next to each word. The correct pronunciations are given in the answers below.

1. ציפור (bird)
2. פרה (cow)
3. בית ספר (school)
4. ספר (book)
5. פה (mouth)
6. פנים (mouth)
7. צהוב (yellow)
8. דצמבר (December)

ANSWERS

1. tsipor
2. para
3. beit sefer
4. sefer
5. pe
6. panim
7. tsahov
8. detsember

UNIT 7 - ק, ע, ח

The letter ח, called khet, is pronounced like the "ch" sound in the German "doch" or the "j" in the Spanish "ojos" (IPA /x/). In Modern Hebrew, ח is pronounced the same as the second pronunciation of כ. This pronunciation will be represented by "kh" in this book. In English this letter is sometimes romanized as "ch".

The letter ע, called ayin, in Modern Hebrew is either pronounced like a glottal stop (IPA /ʔ/) or is silent. Therefore it functions basically the same as א. When there is a glottal stop, it will be represented by ' in the pronunciation in this book.

The letter ק, called qof, is pronounced like the "k" sound in "kick" (IPA /k/). In Modern Hebrew ק is pronounced the same as the first pronunciation of כ.

TRY NOT TO CONFUSE

The letter ה, called he from Unit 3, resembles the new letter khet ח. The difference is that he has a small space between the left stroke and the top of the letter whereas khet is connected. Remember ה is pronounced "h" and ח is pronounced "kh".

The new letter ע resembles the letter צ from Unit 6. Pay close attention to the bottom of each letter to not confuse them. Remember צ is pronounced "ts" and ע is pronounced as either a glottal stop or is silent.

PRACTICE

Try to read these Hebrew words. The English translation is given next to each word. The correct pronunciations are given in the answers below.

1. חזיר (pig)
2. אח (brother)
3. אחות (sister)
4. חנות (shop)
5. חלון (window)
6. כובע (hat)
7. נעל (shoe)
8. עצם (bone)
9. זקן (beard)
10. ירוק (green)
11. קרח (ice)
12. קטן (small)

ANSWERS

1. khazir
2. akh
3. akhot
4. khanut
5. khalon
6. kova
7. na'al
8. etsem
9. zakan
10. yarok
11. kerakh
12. katan

UNIT 8 - REVIEW

PRACTICE 1

Review the previous lessons by reading these real Hebrew place names below. The correct pronunciations are given in the answers below.

1. ישראל
2. ירושלים
3. תל־אביב
4. חיפה
5. באר שבע
6. בני ברק
7. ים המלח
8. ים כנרת
9. נהר הירדן
10. הר הארי

ANSWERS 1

1. Yisra'el (Israel)
2. Yerushalayim (Jerusalem)
3. Tel Aviv
4. Haifa
5. Be'er Sheva (Beersheba)
6. B'nei Brak
7. Yam HaMelakh (Dead Sea)
8. Yam Kinneret (Sea of Galilee)
9. Nahar Hayarden (Jordan River)
10. Har HaAri

PRACTICE 2

Review what you have learned in this book by reading the Hebrew names below. The correct pronunciations are given in the Answers below.

1. בנימין נתניהו
2. שמעון פרס
3. אריאל שרון
4. אהוד ברק
5. יצחק רבין

ANSWERS 2

1. Benyamin Netanyahu
2. Shimon Peres
3. Ariel Sharon
4. Ehud Barak
5. Yitskhak Rabin

APPENDIX - VOWELS

As we have seen, short vowels are not normally written in Modern Israeli Hebrew, except for some special cases, such as dictionaries, poetry and texts for children. Students of Hebrew must therefore get accustomed to reading without the vowel marking as this is the natural way for Modern Hebrew to be written.

When they are shown, vowels are indicated in Hebrew by small dots or bars written either above or below the Hebrew letter. These marks are called niqqud in Hebrew. A comprehensive review of all of the niqqud is beyond the scope of this book and unnecessary for beginners since niqqud are not normally written at all in Modern Hebrew.

Some niqqud that a student may occasionally see in Modern Hebrew are presented below, along with the name and the pronunciation in square brackets. Note that several niqqud are pronounced identically in Modern Israeli Hebrew.

בּ	Patach	[a]
בָּ	Kamatz gadol	[a]
בֲּ	Hataf patach	[a]
בְּ	Sh'va	[e] or [']
בֶּ	Segol	[e]
בֵּ	Zeire	[e]
בֱּ	Hataf segol	[e]
בִּ	Hiriq	[i]
בֹּ	Holam	[o]
בֳּ	Hataf kamatz	[o]
בֻּ	Kubutz	[u]

HEBREW ALPHABET

Letter	Name	Pronunciation
א	Alef	[a]
ב	Bet	[b] / [v]
ג	Gimel	[g]
ד	Dalet	[d]
ה	He	[h]
ו	Vav	[v] / [u] / [o]
ז	Zayin	[z]
ח	Khet	[kh]
ט	Tet	[t]
י	Yod	[y] / [i]
כ	Kaf	[k] / [kh]
ך	Kaf sofit	[kh]
ל	Lamed	[l]
מ	Mem	[m]
ם	Mem sofit	[m]

נ	Nun	[n]
ן	Nun sofit	[n]
ס	Samekh	[s]
ע	Ayin	[']
פ	Pe	[p] / [f]
ף	Pe sofit	[f]
צ	Tsadi	[ts]
ץ	Tsadi sofit	[ts]
ק	Qof	[k]
ר	Resh	[r]
ש	Shin	[sh] / [s]
ת	Tav	[t]

GLOSSARY – THEMATIC ORDER

ANIMALS

בעל חיים	[ba'al khayim]	animal
כלב	[kelev]	dog
חתול	[khatul]	cat
דג	[dag]	fish
ציפור	[tsipor]	bird
פרה	[para]	cow
חזיר	[khazir]	pig
עכבר	[akhbar]	mouse
סוס	[sus]	horse

PEOPLE

בן אדם	[ben adam]	person
אם	[em]	mother
אמא	[imam]	mommy
אב	[av]	father
אבא	[aba]	daddy
בן	[ben]	son
בת	[bat]	daughter
אח	[akh]	brother
אחות	[akhot]	sister
ידיד	[yadid]	friend
אדם	[adam]	man
אשה	[isha]	woman

ילד	[yeled]	boy
ילדה	[yalda]	girl

TRANSPORTATION

רכבת	[rekevet]	train
מטוס	[matos]	airplane
מכונית	[m'khonit]	car (automobile)
אופניים	[ofanayim]	bicycle
אוטובוס	[otobus]	bus
סירה	[sira]	boat

LOCATION

עיר	['ir]	city
בית	[bayit]	house
רחוב	[rekhov]	street
נמל תעופה	[n'mal-t'ufa]	airport
מלון	[malon]	hotel
מסעדה	[mis'ada]	restaurant
בית ספר	[beit sefer]	school
אוניברסיטה	[universita]	university
פרק	[park]	park
חנות	[khanut]	store / shop
בית חולים	[beit kholim]	hospital
כנסייה	[knesia]	church
בית כנסת	[beit k'neset]	synagogue
בנק	[bank]	bank
שוק	[shuk]	market

HOME

שולחן	[shulkhan]	table
כיסא	[kise]	chair
חלון	[khalon]	window
דלת	[delet]	door
ספר	[sefer]	book

CLOTHING

בגדים	[b'gadim]	clothing
כובע	[kova]	hat
שמלה	[simla]	dress
חולצה	[khultsa]	shirt
מכנסיים	[mikhnasayim]	pants
נעל	[na'al]	shoe

BODY

גוף	[guf]	body
ראש	[rosh]	head
פנים	[panim]	face
שערה	[sa'ara]	hair
עין	[ayin]	eye
פה	[pe]	mouth
אף	[af]	nose
אוזן	[ozen]	ear
יד	[yad]	hand / arm
רגל	[regel]	foot / leg

לב	[lev]	heart
דם	[dam]	blood
עצם	[etsem]	bone
זקן	[zakan]	beard

MISCELLANEOUS

כן	[ken]	**yes**
לא	[lo]	**no**
זכ	[ken]	yes
אל	[lo]	no

FOOD & DRINK

אוכל	[okhel]	food
בשר	[basar]	meat
לחם	[lekhem]	bread
גבינה	[g'vina]	cheese
תפוח	[tapuakh]	apple
מים	[mayim]	water
בירה	[bira]	beer
יין	[yayin]	wine
קפה	[kafe]	coffee
תה	[te]	tea
חלב	[khalav]	milk
ארוחת בוקר	[arukhat boker]	breakfast
ארוחת צהריים	[arukhat tsohorayim]	lunch
ארוחת ערב	[arukhat erev]	dinner

COLORS

צבע	[tseva]	color
אדום	[adom]	red
כחול	[kakhol]	blue
ירוק	[yarok]	green
צהוב	[tsahov]	yellow
שחור	[shakhor]	black
לבן	[lavan]	white

NATURE

ים	[yam]	sea
נהר	[nahar]	river
אגם	[agam]	lake
הר	[har]	mountain
גשם	[geshem]	rain
שלג	[sheleg]	snow
עץ	[ets]	tree
פרח	[perakh]	flower
שמש	[shemesh]	sun
ירח	[yareakh]	moon
רוח	[ruakh]	wind
שמים	[shamayim]	sky
אש	[esh]	fire
קרח	[kerakh]	ice

ADJECTIVES

גדול	[gadol]	big
קטן	[katan]	small
טוב	[tov]	good
רע	[ra]	bad
חם	[kham]	hot
קר	[kar]	cold
זול	[zol]	cheap
יקר	[yakar]	expensive
מאושר	[m'ushar]	happy
עצוב	[atzuv]	sad

NUMBERS

אחת	[akhat]	one
שתיים	[sh'tayim]	two
שלוש	[shalosh]	three
ארבע	[arba]	four
חמש	[khamesh]	five
שש	[shesh]	six
שבע	[sheva]	seven
שמונה	[shmone]	eight
תשע	[teisha]	nine
עשר	[eser]	ten

TIME

יום	[yom]	day
חודש	[khodesh]	month
שנה	[shana]	year
שעה	[sha'a]	hour
היום	[ha-yom]	today
מחר	[makhar]	tomorrow
אתמול	[etmol]	yesterday

DAYS OF THE WEEK

יום ראשון	[yom rishon]	Sunday
יום שני	[yom sheni]	Monday
יום שלישי	[yom sh'lishi]	Tuesday
יום רביעי	[yom r'vi'i]	Wednesday
יום חמישי	[yom khamishi]	Thursday
יום שישי	[yom shishi]	Friday
יום שבת	[yom shabat]	Saturday

MONTHS (GREGORIAN)

ינואר	[yanuar]	January
פברואר	[februar]	February
מרץ	[merts]	March
אפריל	[april]	April
מאי	[may]	May
יוני	[yuni]	June
יולי	[yuli]	July

אוגוסט	[ogust]	August
ספטמבר	[september]	September
אוקטובר	[oktober]	October
נובמבר	[november]	November
דצמבר	[detsember]	December

PROPER NAMES

ישראל	[yisra'el]	Israel
ישראלי	[yisra'eli]	Israeli
עברי	[ivri]	Hebrew (language)
יהדות	[yahadut]	Judaism
יהודי	[y'hudi]	Jewish
ירושלים	[yerushalayim]	Jerusalem

GLOSSARY – ALPHABETICAL ORDER

– א –

אב	[av]	father
אבא	[aba]	daddy
אגם	[agam]	lake
אדום	[adom]	red
אדם	[adam]	man
אוגוסט	[ogust]	August
אוזן	[ozen]	ear
אוטובוס	[otobus]	bus
אוכל	[okhel]	food
אוניברסיטה	[universita]	university
אופניים	[ofanayim]	bicycle
אוקטובר	[oktober]	October
אח	[akh]	brother
אחות	[akhot]	sister
אחת	[akhat]	one
אם	[em]	mother
אמא	[imma]	mommy
אף	[af]	nose
אפריל	[april]	April
ארבע	[arba]	four
ארוחת ערב	[arukat erev]	dinner
ארוחת צהריים	[arukhat tsohorayim]	lunch
ארוחת בוקר	[arukhat boker]	breakfast
אש	[esh]	fire

אשה	[isha]	woman
אתמול	[etmol]	yesterday

– ב –

בגדים	[b'gadim]	clothing
בירה	[bira]	beer
בית	[bayit]	house
בית חולים	[beit kholim]	hospital
בית כנסת	[beit k'neset]	synagogue
בית ספר	[beit sefer]	school
בן	[ben]	son
בן אדם	[ben adam]	person
בנק	[bank]	bank
בעל חיים	[baʿal khayim]	animal
בשר	[basar]	meat
בת	[bat]	daughter

– ג –

גבינה	[g'vina]	cheese
גדול	[gadol]	big
גוף	[guf]	body
גשם	[geshem]	rain

– ד –

דג	[dag]	fish
דלת	[delet]	door
דם	[dam]	blood
דצמבר	[detsember]	December

– ה –

היום	[ha-yom]	today
הר	[har]	mountain

– ז –

זול	[zol]	cheap
זקן	[zakan]	beard

– ח –

חודש	[khodesh]	month
חולצה	[khultsa]	shirt
חזיר	[khazir]	pig
חלב	[khalav]	milk
חלון	[khalon]	window
חם	[kham]	hot
חמש	[khamesh]	five
חנוכה	[khanuka]	Hanukkah

חנות	[khanut]	store / shop
חתול	[khatul]	cat

– ט –

טוב	[tov]	good

– י –

יד	[yad]	hand / arm
ידיד	[yadid]	friend
יהדות	[yahadut]	Judaism
יהודי	[y'hudi]	Jewish
יולי	[yuli]	July
יום	[yom]	day
יום חמישי	[yom khamishi]	Thursday
יום כיפור	[yom kipur]	Yom Kippur
יום ראשון	[yom rishon]	Sunday
יום רביעי	[yom r'vi'i]	Wednesday
יום שבת	[yom shabat]	Saturday
יום שישי	[yom shishi]	Friday
יום שלישי	[yom sh'lishi]	Tuesday
יום שני	[yom sheni]	Monday
יוני	[yuni]	June
יין	[yayin]	wine
ילד	[yeled]	boy
ילדה	[yalda]	girl
ים	[yam]	sea
ינואר	[yanuar]	January

יקר	[yakar]	expensive
ירוק	[yarok]	green
ירושלים	[yerushalayim]	Jerusalem
ירח	[yareakh]	moon
ישראל	[yisra'el]	Israel
ישראלי	[yisr'eli]	Israeli

– כ –

כובע	[kova]	hat
כחול	[kakhol]	blue
כיסא	[kise]	chair
כלב	[kelev]	dog
כן	[ken]	yes
כנסייה	[knesia]	church

– ל –

לא	[lo]	no
לב	[lev]	heart
לבן	[lavan]	white
לחם	[lekhem]	bread

– מ –

מאושר	[m'ushar]	happy
מאי	[may]	May
מחר	[makhar]	tomorrow

מטוס	[matos]	airplane
מים	[mayim]	water
מכונית	[m'khonit]	car (automobile)
מכנסיים	[mikhnasayim]	pants
מלון	[malon]	hotel
מסעדה	[mis'ada]	restaurant
מרץ	[merts]	March

– נ –

נהר	[nahar]	river
נובמבר	[november]	November
נמל תעופה	[n'mal-t'ufa]	airport
נעל	[na'al]	shoe

– ס –

סוס	[sus]	horse
סירה	[sira]	boat
ספטמבר	[september]	September
ספר	[sefer]	book

– ע –

עברי	[ivri]	Hebrew
עין	[ayin]	eye
עיר	['ir]	city
עכבר	[akhbar]	mouse

עץ	[ets]	tree
עצוב	[atzuv]	sad
עצם	[etsem]	bone
עשר	[eser]	ten

– פ –

פברואר	[februar]	February
פה	[pe]	mouth
פנים	[panim]	face
פרה	[para]	cow
פרח	[perakh]	flower
פרק	[park]	park

– צ –

צבע	[tseva]	color
צהוב	[tsahov]	yellow
ציפור	[tsipor]	bird

– ק –

קטן	[katan]	small
קפה	[kafe]	coffee
קר	[kar]	cold
קרח	[kerakh]	ice

– ר –

ראש	[rosh]	head
ראש השנה	[rosh hashanah]	Rosh Hashanah
רגל	[regel]	foot / leg
רוח	[ruakh]	wind
רחוב	[rekhov]	street
רכבת	[rekevet]	train
רע	[ra]	bad

– ש –

שבע	[sheva]	seven
שולחן	[shulkhan]	table
שוק	[shuk]	market
שחור	[shakhor]	black
שלג	[sheleg]	snow
שלוש	[shalosh]	three
שמונה	[shmone]	eight
שמים	[shamayim]	sky
שמלה	[simla]	dress
שמש	[shemesh]	sun
שנה	[shana]	year
שעה	[sha'a]	hour
שערה	[sa'ara]	hair
שש	[shesh]	six
שתיים	[sh'tayim]	two

– ת –

תה	[te]	tea
תל אביב	[tel aviv]	Tel Aviv
תפוח	[tapuakh]	apple
תשע	[teisha]	nine

Other language learning titles available from Wolfedale Press:

Learn to Read Arabic in 5 Days
Learn to Read Armenian in 5 Days
Learn to Read Bulgarian in 5 Days
Learn to Read Georgian in 5 Days
Learn to Read Greek in 5 Days
Learn to Read Persian (Farsi) in 5 Days
Learn to Read Russian in 5 Days
Learn to Read Ukrainian in 5 Days